SHEDWORDS

SHEDWORDS

100 RARE WORDS TO EXPLORE AND ENJOY

Rob Smith

CORWIN

A SAGE company
2455 Teller Road
Thousand Oaks, California 91320
(0800)233-9936
www.corwin.com

SAGE Publications Ltd
1 Oliver's Yard
55 City Road
London EC1Y 1SP

SAGE Publications India Pvt Ltd
B 1/I 1 Mohan Cooperative Industrial Area
Mathura Road
New Delhi 110 044

SAGE Publications Asia-Pacific Pte Ltd
3 Church Street
#10-04 Samsung Hub
Singapore 049483

Editor: Amy Thornton
Senior project editor: Chris Marke
Marketing Manager: Dilhara Attygalle
Cover design: Wendy Scott
Typeset by: C&M Digitals (P) Ltd, Chennai, India
Printed in the UK

Library of Congress Control Number: 2020951797

British Library Cataloguing in Publication Data

ISBN 978-1-5297-2993-1
ISBN 978-1-5297-2992-4 (pbk)

At SAGE we take sustainability seriously. Most of our products are printed in the UK using responsibly sourced papers and boards. When we print overseas we ensure sustainable papers are used as measured by the PREPS grading system. We undertake an annual audit to monitor our sustainability.

CONTENTS

ABOUT THE AUTHOR

Rob Smith was born in Widnes, where he spent his youth playing rugby, before leaving to attend Northampton University to study Primary Education. Upon graduating, Rob began his teaching career in Kettering before moving back to his native North West, teaching in schools in Heywood and Manchester. Rob began to introduce short films into his writing lessons from the outset. These ranged from movie trailers to animated shorts and included offerings from the BFI and IntoFilm. Rob has always firmly believed that film has an incredibly important place within the classroom. Film gives children experiences of people and places that they may not have encountered before. Film has the ability to take viewers from the depths of the deepest oceans, into the jungles and deserts across the planet and then blast them into deep space and beyond. Film can send viewers back to the dawn of time and transport us into an imagined future. It is these experiences that Rob was able to tap into and fire the imagination of his students.

Rob created The Literacy Shed in order to store and share the film shorts. It became hugely popular with teachers and was very quickly used all around the world. Rob then started to visit schools to share how film could be used effectively in English lessons.

Rob now lives near Bury with his partner, Katherine, their three sons and a border terrier called Myrtle. He spends his time creating teaching materials, delivering teacher training, writing books and building Lego.

ABOUT THIS BOOK

Words have been created since the dawn of time when people first started to communicate and name things. Through the ages, words have drifted in and out of regular usage for one reason or another. It is this constant ebb and flow of words, and their popularity, that keeps English in a constant state of flux. Often, popular culture can play a role in this. From Shakespeare introducing words such as 'dauntless' and 'lonely', Milton's 'pandemonium' and Lewis Carroll's 'chortle', authors have been able to add to our lexicon, and now modern culture has given us words like 'emoji', 'bromance' and 'fatberg'. These are all very 'buzzworthy'; however, the birth of new words can sound the death knell for older words.

In this book, I have attempted to breathe some new life into words which are rarely used or have already dropped out of common usage. But, why? As a teacher, I have always enjoyed sharing new words with students and engendering a love of language. When The Literacy Shed came into being, its social media offered a wider platform for sharing the words, and #ShedWords was born.

I spent many hours, in my spare time, searching for unusual words, and sharing, in my opinion, the most beautiful or interesting of them with an illustrative sentence, a definition and a striking image. People enjoyed them and I shared more, before having a discussion with my editor Amy Thornton at SAGE Publishing about the opportunity to turn this collection into a book. This is the culmination of that conversation and about two years' worth of emails.

I should point out that this book is not an exhaustive list of great words to introduce to children. Neither is it a list of words that MUST be shared with all pupils to help them succeed or increase their vocabulary. It is important to understand that, if used too frequently, the words can overwhelm the reader, slow the reading and thus spoil the reading experience. Careful selection and precision of placement is key: these words should not be forced into a sentence where their splendour becomes muted.

So how might the book be used? Teachers may want to introduce a 'word of the week' to their students, and the words contained herein may be worthy candidates. Each page can be used as a writing prompt with the students encouraged to write about the image. whilst incorporating the ShedWord. The words might also be researched and their etymology studied. Ultimately, the book can be used in a variety of ways, but students need to understand that these words, used sparingly, can add a speck of beauty to their writing. It is a treasury of words from which glittering jewels can be plucked by those who will admire them most and who will use them to adorn speech and writing only where they will sit best. If nothing else, I hope the book will kindle an interest in less-familiar vocabulary and revive some long-forgotten words that have become lost in the vaults of time.

Follow @LiteracyShed on Twitter and Instagram to see further ShedWord examples or search for the #ShedWords hashtag to see more examples.

For my Mum and Dad

adumbral

Adjective: *shadowy*

At dusk, in the adumbral forest, a figure crept slowly towards the mouth of the cave.

From Latin *adumbrates*, meaning to cast a shadow over.

3

advesperate

Verb: *to darken or to draw towards evening*

The day began to advesperate: the sky darkened, workers hurried home, fires were lit and curtains were drawn.

Another word borrowed from Latin: *ad* means to or towards and *vesper* is an archaic word for evening.

aestivation

Noun: *a period of dormancy which takes place in the summer; the opposite of the more commonly known 'hibernation' which is a period of dormancy that takes place during winter*

The Malagasy fat-tailed dwarf lemur and the East African hedgehog go into aestivation for several months of the year.

amaranthine

Adjective: *undying; immortal; eternally beautiful*

Beauty lay on a soft bed in the highest tower of the castle. The wicked witch had cast her into amaranthine slumber.

The amaranth is the undying flower of Aesop's fable.

ammil

Noun: *a glistening film of ice that covers twigs, leaves and grass after a freeze*

The light caught the ammil, which sheathed every surface, and in the early morning sunshine a glittering splendour shone across the valley.

From *amel*, an Old English word for enamel.

amorphous

Adjective: *without a clear shape or structure*

A dark amorphous shadow filled the room and suddenly everyone was cold.

appetency

Noun: *a longing or desire*

His greatest appetency was to be accepted into the secret conclave. Would they let him in?

A synonym of appetite, craving, desire, drive, hunger, lust and yearning.

apricity

Noun: *the warmth of the sun on a cold day*

The sun broke through the clouds offering a few moments of apricity to warm their bones.

The verb form is to apricate, which means 'to bask in the sun'.

araneous

Adjective: *transparent; delicate; like a cobweb*

The araneous veil between the two realms was split and creatures were climbing through from another dimension.

From the Latin *aranea*, meaning spider.

arcadian

Adjective: *idyllic and serene, often used to describe pastoral scenes; can be used as a noun to describe someone who lives a simple life without the hustle and bustle of the city*

As the rain came down, the shepherd sheltered against the worst of it inside her shelter and looked out over the tranquil arcadian scene which stretched out before her.

In Greek mythology, Arcadia was the wilderness home of Pan who lived there with the nymphs and dryads.

argentous

Adjective: *silver in colour*

The argentous-haired man towered over him, grinning malevolently.

aureate

Adjective: *gold in colour*

Aureate light shone down, illuminating the surface of the ocean and causing golden ripples all the way to the horizon.

bombinate

Verb: *to make a humming or buzzing sound*

The air around them began to crackle and bombinate as if filled with a magical energy.

From the Greek *bómbos*, meaning any deep, hollow sound or humming, buzzing, booming and rumbling. So this means that the gentle 'bumble' of the bee and the destructive booming of a bomb have the same linguistic roots.

bosky

Adjective: *having an abundancy of trees or shrubs; relating to woodland*

The girls looked along the path through the wildflower meadows and into the bosky surroundings.

brivet

Verb: *to wander without purpose; to look through items often in an illicit or furtive manner*

They waited for him to leave and then clambered through the windows before beginning to brivet around.

Brobdingnagian

Adjective: *gigantic; huge; colossal*

The steam engine towered above them so Brobdingnagian in its proportions that they could barely see past the tender to the carriages beyond.

In Jonathan Swift's famous tale from 1726, Gulliver visits Lilliput, an island of minute people; later, he visits Brobdingnag, an island inhabited by giants and thus everything on the island is gigantic.

brontide

Noun: *a sound like the distant rumble of thunder*

Dense clouds sprawled across the sky and the air grew heavy. A flash of silver briefly lit up the sky before a brontide rolled across the rooftops and then came the pitter-patter of raindrops on the slate roofs of the houses.

Probably from the Greek noun *brontē*, meaning thunder, with the suffix '-ide', meaning offspring of. We also see *brontē* in the word Brontosaurus, the thunder lizard.

brumous

Adjective: *of grey skies and wintry days; heavy cloud or fog; a period of cold and sunless weather*

The colours of the autumnal trees were diminished by the brumous wrappings of a wintry dawn.

Related: brumal, an adjective meaning 'belonging to winter' – e.g. the *brumal* animals were transformed as their coats changed from brown to white.

calescent

Adjective: *becoming warmer or hotter*

After hearing the news, calescent anger formed inside him and threatened to burst out.

caliginous

Adjective: *dark; dim; gloomy*

The moon shone through the cracked, stained-glass windows, casting muted colours into the caliginous interior of the long-abandoned chapel.

candescent

Adjective: *glowing with heat, illuminated*

The candescent glow of their campfire flicked shadows around the trees that surrounded them.

From the Latin verb *candere*, to glow, prevalent in the early nineteenth century to describe the light emitted from gas lanterns.

cerulean

Adjective: *deep blue in colour, often associated with the sky*

With a swish of her tail, she disappeared beneath the waves and headed down into the cerulean depths.

clandestine

Adjective: *Secretive; shady; something that takes place in the shadows or under the cover of darkness*

The clandestine group had decided to meet at midnight to discuss their plans for revenge.

constellate

Verb: *To form a cluster; group or gather together*

The villagers began to constellate in the stalls of the night market to share food and stories

contumacious

Adjective: *stubborn; rebellious*

She stood in the headteacher's study leaning in a contumacious way against the chair, awaiting her punishment.

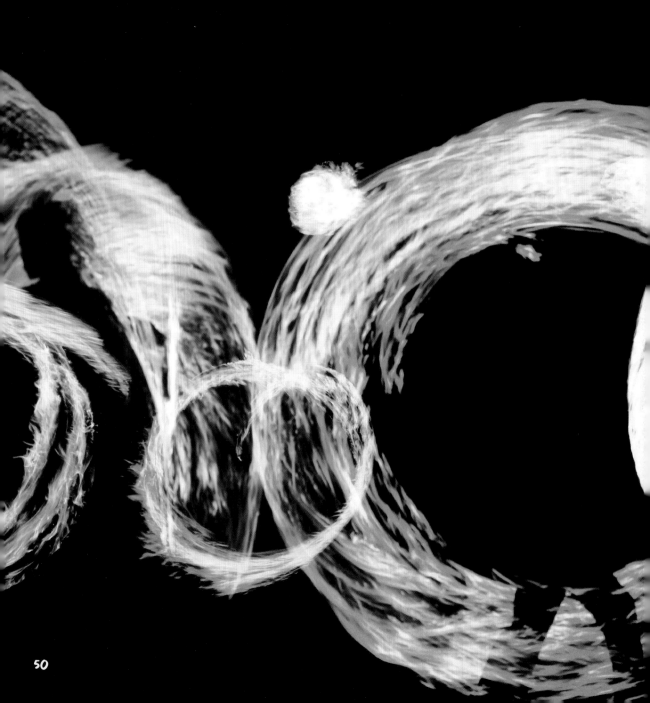

50

coruscate

Verb: *to flash or sparkle*

The power began to coruscate within him; it shone like a halo all around him and then the lightning erupted from his palms towards his nemesis.

crepuscular

Adjective: *relating to or resembling twilight*

The figure stood before her in the crepuscular hallway. A light flashed momentarily and it was then that she recognised him.

Also used in biology to describe those creatures who emerge at dusk. Crepuscular creatures include hedgehogs and bats.

deliciate

Verb: *luxuriate; to take personal pleasure; to revel; to enjoy oneself; feast; indulge in delights*

The emperor would deliciate in the spectacle of the games which climaxed in death and gore.

58

desuetude

Noun: *no longer active; a state of disuse*

The abbey fell into a state of desuetude following King Henry's dissolution of the monasteries.

diaphanous

Adjective: *very delicate and thin; translucent*

A kaleidoscope of butterflies wafted past, fluttering their diaphanous wings delicately.

First used in English in the seventeenth century after a journey from Greek through medieval Latin.

dolorous

Adjective: *feeling or expressing great sorrow; sorrowful*

The dolorous creature sat and surveyed the destruction all around her.

06:35

dreich

Adjective, borrowed from Scots: *bleak and dreary weather*

It was a dreich landscape; lights struggled to break through the gloom that enveloped the city.

effulgence

Noun: *brilliant radiance shining forth*

The sun climbed above the horizon, its effulgence lighting up the morning sky.

egregious

Adjective: *Outrageous; shocking or outstandingly bad*

He told an egregious lie; the consequences were far-reaching and terrible for many.

eidolan

Noun: *spirit; phantom; apparition; a shade of the human form*

Under the full moon, he heard the church clock strike midnight. A figure stood before him, unsubstantial, an eidolan dressed in unfamiliar clothing.

eldritch

Adjective: *weird and sinister; ghostly*

Daring each other, the two of them crept along the pathway that ran through the eldritch forest towards the abandoned shack at its centre.

Elysian

Adjective: *gloriously blissful; delightful*

Running through the sun-dappled glade, the stream splashed its crystal-clear waters over the rocks in this Elysian landscape.

In Greek mythology, Elysium or the Elysian Fields were the final resting place of the fallen heroes. Probably first used as an adjective by Samuel Johnson.

empyrean

Adjective: *Heavenly; awe inspiring*

The waves towered above the boat like empyrean beings reaching to the skies.

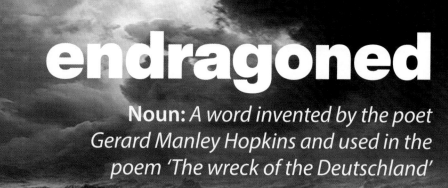

endragoned

Noun: *A word invented by the poet Gerard Manley Hopkins and used in the poem 'The wreck of the Deutschland'*

The ship was tossed and rolled by endragoned seas.

ethereous

Adjective: *made of or resembling ether; ethereal*

Dusk descended. As they crossed the clearing, an owl swooped in ethereous flight; almost silently the ghostly creature came and then left as quietly as it came.

facinorous

Adjective: *extremely wicked*

Their facinorous stepmother banished them to the forest.

feuillemort

Adjective: *the colour of dying or faded leaves, literally from the French morte – dead – and feuille – leaf*

As the summer turned to autumn, the earth grew cooler and the feuillemort colours took hold of the forest.

flexuous

Adjective: *having curves, bends or turns; undulating and twisting*

Flexuous vines hung from the tree's branches twisting themselves around its immense trunk.

From the Latin *flexus*, meaning the act of bending.

flocculent

Adjective: *resembling wool; soft and fluffy in appearance*

In the cobalt sky, flocculent clouds cast lazy shadows on the landscape below.

90

foliage

Noun: *collectively, the leaves of one or more plants*

The sunlight shone through the foliage overhead and dappled the verdant glade below.

First recorded use: 1580.

foudroyant

Adjective: *sudden and overwhelming; stunning; dazzling; as if struck by lightning*

Lightning struck the forest and foudroyant flames enveloped the ancient oak tree standing in the glade.

fugacious

Adjective: *lasting only a short time; fleeting; tending to disappear*

The fugacious colours of the rainbow softened and then drifted away as the sky clouded over.

fuliginous

Adjective: *sooty; dark; obscure; murky*

A fuliginous cloud descended on the city. People scuttled into their homes and locked their doors. Upstairs, children did not dare to peak through their windows.

From *fuligo*, the late Latin word for soot. It can also be used to describe something as dark or murky in the sense of being purposefully vague or obscure.

gallimaufry

Noun: *a confused jumble or medley of things*

The junkyard stretched out ahead of them. A huge gallimaufry of gaskets, coils and tyres. It would take hours to find what they were looking for.

gloaming

Noun: *the time after the sun goes down before darkness falls completely*

At gloaming, the night sky began to darken. It was neither day time nor night time, but that magical time between when twilight had arrived.

This word almost died out in English except in some Northern regional dialects. However, it was brought back into usage by some poets, most notably Robert Burns who uses it in *I'll Meet Thee On The Lea Rig*.

Gie me the hour o' gloamin' grey,
It maks my heart to sae cheery O.
To meet thee on the lea-rig,
My ain kind Dearie O.

gossamer

Adjective: *thin and light; almost see-through*

The spider spun its gossamer thread throughout the night and by morning the delicate grey fairy-cloak was spread across the space where the window had been.

illecebrous

Adjective: *enticing*

They looked through the window at the long illecebrous garden that led away from the house down to the magical woodlands beyond.

ineffable

Adjective: *too great to be described in words*

The vast white wilderness stretched out before them, its ineffable size and emptiness filling each of the explorers with a sense of apprehension and exhilaration.

From Latin, *ineffabilis*, meaning unutterable; ineffable means that something is so powerful that it renders the viewer speechless.

ineluctable

Adjective: *inescapable; impossible to avoid*

From the moment he was born, the prophecies showed that his destiny was ineluctable.

jaculiferous

Adjective: *prickly or bearing spines*

A porcupine could be described as jaculiferous, but I would like the usage to include those people with prickly personalities. The teenage girl had woken up late and spent the morning in a jaculiferous mood, snapping at anyone who dared to talk to her.

120

labyrinthine

Adjective: *like a maze; complex; complicated and confusing*

The narrow labyrinthine streets of the ancient city made it almost impossible to follow the guide.

lambent

Adjective: *glowing; gleaming; a soft flickering*

The lambent light of the evening sun lingered in the sky, painting it a rich shade of orange while pink clouds dotted the firmament.

lapidose

Adjective: *stony or having an abundance of stone*

The dry lapidose ground meant that not many plants grew across the tundra which stretched for miles.

It is easy to imagine someone with a cruel, lapidose heart: the wicked queen in *Snow White*, for example.

lassitude

Noun: *a state of weariness; mentally tired; lacking energy*

Afterwards, he was afflicted with an unconquerable lassitude, which led him to slump in his chair. If he ever had to go through that again then it would be too soon.

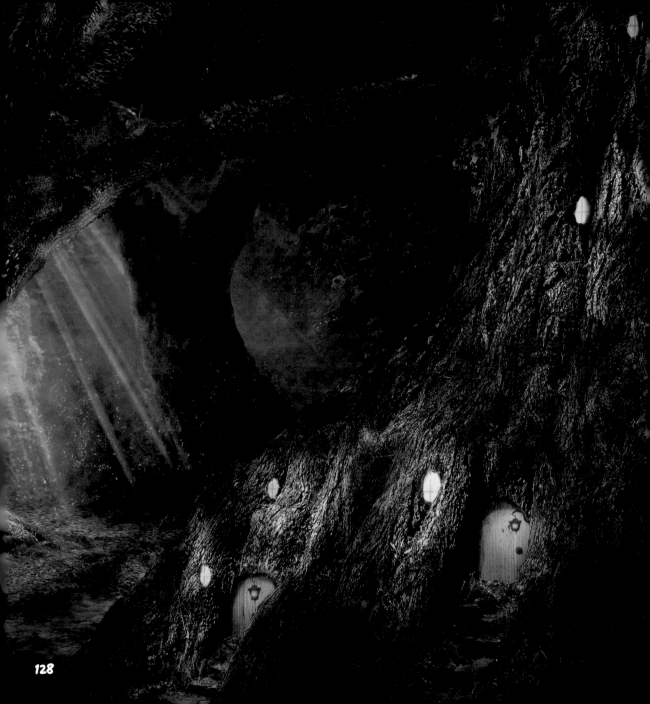

latibule

Noun: *hiding place; place of safety and comfort*

He ran into the woods towards his latibule high in the trees where he knew he wouldn't be found.

lissome

Adjective: *nimble; agile; flexible*

The lissome dancer rose up into the shower of droplets as if he were about to fly.

machination

Noun: *a plot or scheme; often crafty or sly in nature*

The group gathered in the shadows to discuss their latest machination. The leader had decided that tonight would be their best chance to capture the young wizard.

magisterial

Adjective: *having or showing great authority*

The monarch stood at the front of the court and demanded silence before issuing magisterial commands to the young courtiers sitting in rows before her.

malagrugrous

Adjective: *dismal; depressing; gloomy*

The carts rattled over the cobbles; all the lights were misty across the river; the sounds of the dock workers were muffled by the fog and this was how the malagrugrous day was to begin.

marmoreal

Adjective: *resembling or made of marble*

His eyes glowed red; his tattered clothes billowed around him and his marmoreal skin began to glow with magical energies.

matutinal

Adjective: *of the morning*

The matutinal chorus signalled the awakening of the birds outside my window.

The word comes from Matuta, the Roman goddess, referred to by the Latin poet Lucretius as the goddess of the dawn. It has the same root as the French word *matin*, meaning morning, and thus morning theatre shows – matinees.

mazarine

Adjective: *a rich blue colour*

He looked into the deep pools of her mazarine eyes and saw a sadness lingering there.

mellifluous

Adjective: *pleasing and musical to the ear*

The mellifluous sound was so real to her that she could close her eyes and picture it as a smooth flow of gently coloured strings.

From Latin *mellifluus*, meaning flowing like honey, so *mellifluous* sounds flow sweetly in your ears.

meracious

Adjective: *undiluted; unadulterated; full strength; pungent*

Her meracious anger was clear for all to see as she swept through the palace doors into the grand ball to which she hadn't been invited.

minatory

Adjective: *threatening*

The room was full so he couldn't get to her. He stood across from her in the crowd and watched. His minatory gaze was unwavering.

moonbroch

Noun: *a word borrowed from Scots, meaning a luminous ring or corona around the moon. This is caused by moonlight reflecting off ice-crystals or moisture in the clouds*

The moonbroch **lit up the sky above the forest so brightly that they could see the path stretching out ahead of them.**

moonglade

Noun: *the track that the moon makes upon the water as it rises*

The moonglade rippled gently on the surface of the black lake, signalling the arrival of the night.

murmurous

Adjective: *characterised by the sound of low, indistinct murmuring*

She peered through the mist and the figures seemed to appear from the vast murmurous forest.

First recorded in 1582, the same year that words such as mismatch, anathema, thunderous, toaster and toughen were also recorded.

niveous

Adjective: *snowy; made of or resembling snow*

The niveous landscape was eerily quiet and the streetlights were illuminated with soft orbs of light.

As well as describing snowy scenes, the word can also be used to describe white objects such as the *niveous* feathers of an owl or the *niveous* skin of a pale maiden.

nocuous

Adjective: *harmful; poisonous*

The door was locked from the outside, the air began to change and a nocuous, yellow gas-cloud was pooling at their feet. Would they escape this time?

A word that is rarely used; however, many people use its antonym 'innocuous'.

orphic

Adjective: *entrancing; mysterious; beyond the normal realms of understanding*

The orphic sounds drifted around the cave, lulling the visitors into a calmness that, if they had known what was lurking beneath the dark waters, would certainly have been replaced by fear.

pallid

Adjective: *pale; lacking vigour*

She saw a pallid face looking back at her through the window. She screamed!

paragon

Noun: *a perfect example of a particular quality or characteristic*

The knight, a paragon of honour and chivalry, kept her promise and released all the prisoners unharmed after the battle.

pellucid

Adjective: *very clear; transparent; shining*

The sky outside the window was a pale pellucid blue with not even a wisp of cloud in sight.

perfidious

Adjective: *untrustworthy; deceitful*

The traitorous spy led a perfidious attack against her former companions.

petrichor

Noun: *the earthy smell that emanates from the ground following rain after a dry spell*

The air was filled with the pleasant petrichor as the sun began to peek through the trees and the rain clouds dissipated.

The word was coined in the 1960s and is constructed from two Greek words: *petra*, meaning rock, and *ichor*, the fluid that flows through the veins of the gods in Greek mythology.

portentous

Noun: *something ominous or threatening; a sign that something bad is on its way*

From that portentous moment, when all the lights flickered and then went out, they knew that they were in trouble.

pulchritude

Noun: *physical beauty*

Cinderella's pulchritude lit up the ballroom, catching the eye of the handsome prince.

pulchritudinous

Adjective: *physically beautiful or attractive*

Some say that pulchritudinous Helen of Troy was the most beautiful woman in the whole world.

181

punctilious

Adjective: *showing great attention to detail*

The squire was punctilious in the care of his master's armour and weapons for he knew that this was a matter of life and death.

From the Italian *pontiglio* through French and then appearing in English in the seventeenth century.

Synonyms: rigorous, particular, sedulous, meticulous, fastidious, conscientious, diligent.

querencia

Noun: *a place from where strength can be drawn*

The gladiator stood in the centre of the arena, a querencia to recover in as the fight raged on all around.

Querencia is a Spanish word with a number of different meanings, ranging from fondness, homing instinct, an animal's den or lair, and also a bull's preferred spot in the bullring.

quiescent

Adjective: *at rest; quiet; dormant; inactive*

In the quiescent moments before dawn, the soldiers huddled in their trenches awaiting the inevitable bombardment that the morning would bring.

192

rampike

Noun: *a dead tree that has remained standing, often with a bleached trunk or damage due to fire or lightning*

Across no man's land, the eerie figures of rampikes stood gnarled and contorted in the mist.

salebrous

Adjective: *rugged; rough*

They travelled along an old salebrous road over the mountains and every step that the horses took made the wagon rock from side to side.

From the Latin *salebra*, meaning a rugged road.

selcouth

Adjective: *unfamiliar; rare; strange and yet still marvellous and wondrous*

Each of the underground passages had been the same but this one was different. The walls shimmered and glistered with mineral deposits; a selcouth sight at the end of the tunnel made them walk on, transfixed.

serein

Noun: *fine rain that falls from a clear sky often at or after sunset*

Long shadows were cast by the trees on the slopes and slowly disappeared as the sun set behind the peaks. The serein then lightly kissed the foliage and left as quickly as it had come.

Serein **conjures up a serene scene.**

sibylline

Adjective: *prophetic; mysterious and often cryptic*

Her sibylline message was scrawled across the stone wall in something that looked like blood. 'Beware, the son of snakes!', it read.

Sibyl was a woman in both Greek and Roman mythology who was said to have the prophetic ability to see into the future.

snowbroth

Noun: *a word which has been in use, albeit rarely, for around 500 years, meaning 'freshly melted snow'*

The mountaineers warmed snowbroth on their paraffin heaters to make tea.

spoondrift

Noun: *the spray blown from the tops of waves by the wind*

As the wind rose, spoondrift was driven across the sands and into the faces of the intrepid beachcombers.

Another word borrowed from Scots, but more commonly known as 'spindrift'.

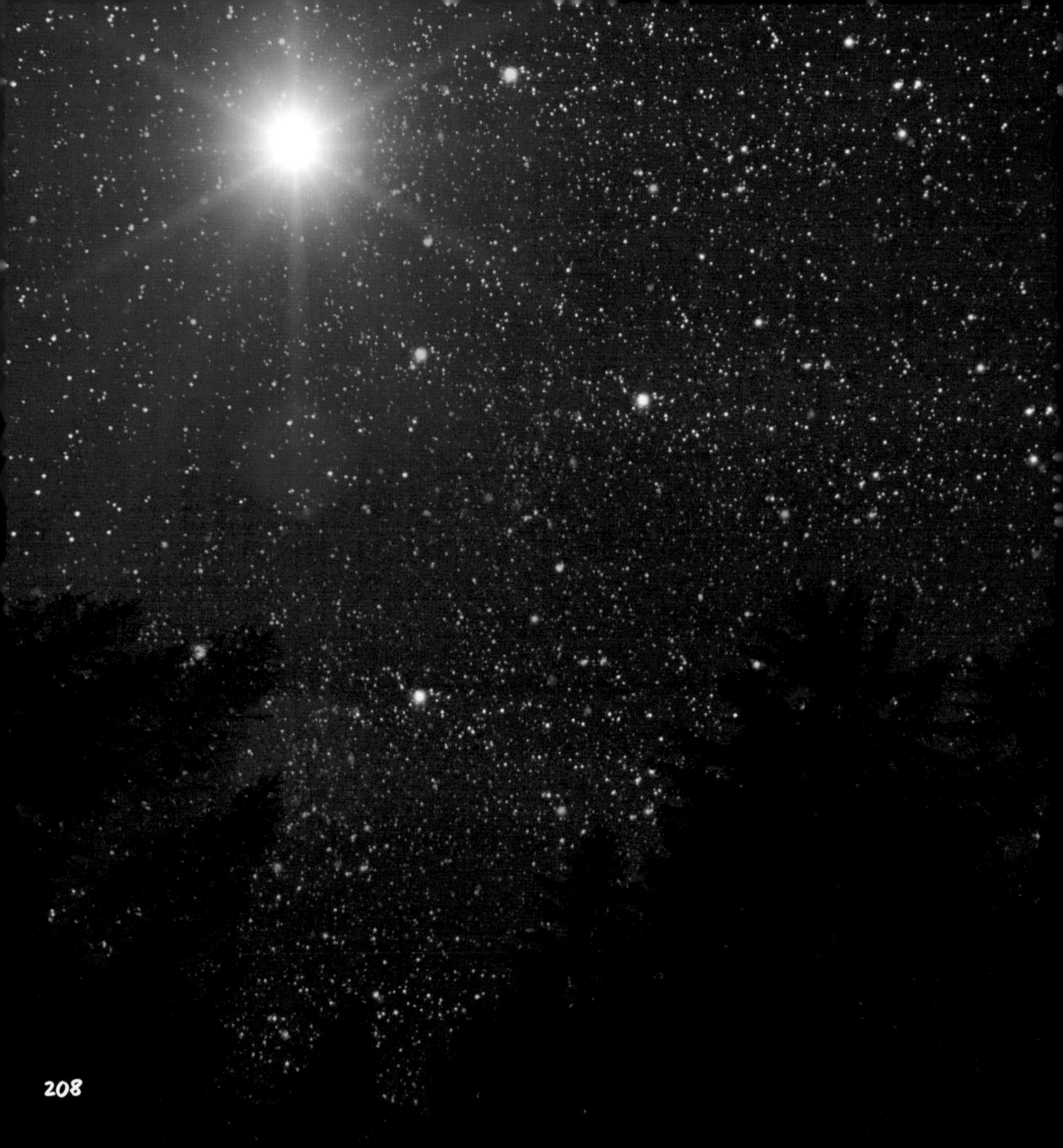

stelliferous

Adjective: *filled with an abundance of stars*

He looked up at the stelliferous sky and marvelled at its vastness. Was there anything out there?

susurrus

Noun: *a whispering or rustling sound*

She stood still, her senses sharpened; she saw the slightest movement on a branch above and heard the susurrus of leaves and then everything went black.

tenebrous

Adjective: *dark; gloomy; shadowy*

Gargoyles stared down from damp stone walls of the castle; high above them lightning flashed and illuminated the tenebrous sky momentarily.

Can also be used as a noun: *tenebrosity*, meaning darkness.

The room was in silent tenebrosity; she took one step inside and waited.

turadh

Noun: *in Scots-Gaelic, turadh is a noun that means a break in the clouds or the dry spell between rain showers*

They had waited for a turadh before beginning their ascent and now there was a break in the clouds.

umbrageous

Adjective: *providing shade*

Sitting under the spreading branches of the umbrageous tree, the ancient traveller rested his weary feet.

vespertine

Adjective: *of the evening; something that happens in or resembles evening*

The moon rose lazily and illuminated the vespertine darkness.

vespine

Adjective: *relating to or resembling wasps*

She was always overtly critical; her vespine tongue had made her seem quite unfriendly to many.

vulpine

Adjective: *from the Latin for fox, vulpes, vulpine is an adjective meaning relating to foxes, but it also describes having fox-like characteristics*

A vulpine smile spread across her face: she had him cornered.

A BOOK TO INSPIRE AND SUPPORT TEACHERS TO EXPLORE AND TEACH AMAZING WORDS.

A resource to widen the vocabulary of teachers and the children they teach.

When children are inspired by words, their literacy learning and engagement in writing can be transformed.

CORWIN
A SAGE Publishing Company

2455 Teller Road | Thousand Oaks, CA 91320
T: (800) 233-9936 | F: (800) 417-2466
www.corwin.com

ISBN 978-1-5297-2992-4

9 781529 729924